CHEERLEADING

CHEER TOOLS AND GEAR

By Carla Mooney

SportsZone
An Imprint of Abdo Publishing
abdobooks.com

abdobooks.com

Printed in the United States of America, North Mankato, Minnesota
052024
092024

Cover Photo: Charles Baus/Cal Sport Media/ZUMA Press Wire/AP Images
Interior Photos: Justin Ford/Getty Images Sport/Getty Images, 4–5; Orlando/Three Lions/Hulton Archive/Getty Images, 6; Amy Lemus/NurPhoto/Getty Images, 8–9; Matthew Pearce/Icon Sportswire/AP Images, 11; B. Christopher/Alamy, 12; Suzi Nelson/Shutterstock Images, 14; Sebastian Gollnow/picture-alliance/dpa/AP Images, 15; Shutterstock Images, 16–17; Phelan M. Ebenhack/AP Images, 19; Stephanie Zollshan/The Berkshire Eagle/AP Images, 20; Taras Grebinets/iStockphoto, 23; Christian Petersen/Getty Images Sport/Getty Images, 24–25; John Cordes/Icon Sportswire/AP Images, 26; Jeffrey Brown/Icon Sportswire, 29

Editor: Christa Kelly
Series Designer: Kate Liestman

Library of Congress Control Number: 2023949390

Library of Congress Cataloging-in-Publication Data

Names: Mooney, Carla, author.
Title: Cheer tools and gear / by Carla Mooney
Description: Minneapolis, Minnesota: Abdo Publishing, 2025 | Series: Cheerleading | Includes online resources and index.
Identifiers: ISBN 9781098293505 (lib. bdg.) | ISBN 9798384912774 (ebook)
Subjects: LCSH: Cheerleading--Juvenile literature. | Tools--Juvenile literature. | Sports--Juvenile literature.
Classification: DDC 791.6--dc23

TABLE OF CONTENTS

CHAPTER 1

DAZZLING THE CROWD

It's game day! As the football players take the field, the cheerleaders line up on the sideline. The cheerleaders wear identical black-and-red uniforms and white sneakers. Their hair is pulled back with matching black bows. They shake shiny black pom-poms.

During the game, the cheerleaders perform sideline chants. Their movements are crisp and coordinated. They dance and entertain the fans sitting in the stands.

More than 250 colleges have cheerleading teams.

OLE MISS REBELS
VS

Cheerleaders have used poms since the 1930s.

Some of the cheerleaders hold up signs with messages such as "Louder," "Noise," and "Defense." The messages help the fans cheer together. The cheerleaders celebrate when the team scores a touchdown.

During halftime, the cheerleaders perform stunts on the field. They lift their teammates high into the air before catching them safely on the ground. They smile up at the crowd as the audience cheers.

Cheerleading is an exciting activity. Cheerleaders can cheer for schools or clubs. Others cheer for professional sports teams. Some cheer teams enter competitions. They compete against other cheer teams in front of judges.

No matter who they cheer with, cheerleaders use special gear and tools to perform. Special uniforms allow them to safely execute impressive skills. Props help draw attention to their sideline cheers and dance routines. Cheerleaders also have gear and tools for training. This gear includes mats and practice clothes. Knowing how to use cheer tools and gear is one of the first steps toward becoming a cheerleader.

CHAPTER 2

CHEER UNIFORMS

Cheerleading teams wear matching uniforms while performing. Uniforms help teams look like a cohesive group. They also help cheerleaders perform their skills safely.

MADE TO MOVE

Modern cheerleading uniforms are made of stretchy materials such as Lycra and spandex. These materials fit close to the body. Loose clothes can get snagged

Cheer uniforms can cost hundreds of dollars.

PIONSHIP

NFC CHAMPIONSHIP
LIONS
WIN

during stunts or tumbling skills, which can cause injuries. Tight uniforms allow cheerleaders to dance, jump, and perform tumbling skills with ease.

The top of a cheerleader's uniform is called a shell. Shells can be made with or without sleeves. In cold weather, a cheerleader may wear a bodysuit or tank top under the shell to stay warm. Many cheer teams also have warm-up jackets.

Uniforms for female cheerleaders often include matching skirts. Cheerleading skirts are short so they do not interfere with movement. Cheerleaders wear cheer briefs under their skirts. Cheer briefs look like shorts. Some briefs have team logos on them. Male cheerleaders often wear pants or shorts that match their tops.

Shoes are an essential part of a cheerleader's uniform. Since cheerleaders perform acrobatic tumbling routines, it helps for their shoes to be lightweight. They must also provide support and cushioning to prevent injuries. Cheerleaders also wear matching socks. Cheer socks are also cushioned. They should also be breathable and absorbent to keep a cheerleader's feet comfortable when performing.

Cheerleading shoes are normally white to stand out against mats and floors.

Some organizations, such as the U.S. All Star Federation, have rules about what kinds of makeup cheerleaders can wear during competitions.

HAIR AND MAKEUP

It's important for cheerleaders to be able to see while performing. Long or unruly hair can cover their eyes and potentially cause problems. Wearing a high ponytail can effectively hold back long hair. Cheerleaders with short hair often use barrettes and headbands to keep their hair out of their faces.

Many cheerleaders use hair spray. This keeps the athletes' hair in place while they are performing.

Some cheerleading squads tie matching bows in their hair. Bows come in all shapes, sizes, and colors. School cheerleaders often wear bows with their school's colors.

Many cheer teams wear matching makeup on game day or competition day. Similar makeup helps the cheerleaders look like one team. A cheerleader's makeup needs to last for hours. It must stay in place through sweat and exercise.

NO JEWELRY

Most cheer teams do not allow members to wear jewelry when practicing or performing. Jewelry is a safety risk. It can get caught on gear or other cheerleaders, causing injuries. Piercings, necklaces, and other jewelry should be removed before performing.

PRACTICE GEAR

Cheerleaders usually practice in everyday exercise clothes. Others have designated practice uniforms. Practice uniforms are often simpler than competition uniforms but still fit tightly to keep the cheerleaders safe as they practice.

Some cheer teams have matching cheer bags. Cheer bags are used to carry clothes, poms, shoes, water bottles, and other gear. They come in different sizes and colors. Some are duffel bags, while others are backpacks. Many cheer bags have a team's

Cheer bags are especially necessary for teams that travel to compete.

Wearing practice uniforms during training keeps the more expensive competition uniforms new and intact.

name or school logo printed on them. Cheer bags can also be customized with a cheerleader's name.

Cheerleaders' attire is an essential part of their gear. Proper clothing helps them stay safe and comfortable. It also helps the squad look like a unified team.

CHAPTER 3

IN THE GYM

Cheerleaders spend a lot of time training in the gym. They exercise to improve their strength, stamina, and flexibility, all while learning new skills and practicing routines. As they train, cheerleaders use special gear to help them safely master new skills.

ESSENTIAL TOOLS

Every cheerleader needs to have a water bottle. Cheerleading is a strenuous

Cheerleaders practice three to five times each week.

activity, and it's important that athletes stay well hydrated while training and performing. Experts recommend that people drink at least eight cups of water every day. More is needed during heavy exercise. Failure to stay hydrated can lead to serious health problems, including fainting and heatstroke.

In addition, teams should always have a first aid kit available. A proper kit has all the necessary supplies to treat injuries that may occur during practice. Supplies should include daily medications for squad members, pain relievers, bandages, tweezers, and triple antibiotic ointment.

MATS AND FLOORS

Cheerleading can be a dangerous activity. However, specially designed mats and floors can help protect cheerleaders as they practice and perform complex skills. Coaches and instructors can teach cheerleaders how to correctly use mats and other safety equipment.

Floor mats are among the most important tools cheerleaders use. Cheerleaders practice jumps, stunts, and tumbling skills on floor mats. These mats are made of foam and provide cushioning, helping prevent injuries during falls. They come in a number

In addition to cushioning falls, many mats also prevent slipping.

of sizes. Some are small, while others may stretch across an entire gym floor.

Landing mats are designed to protect cheerleaders as they practice stunts, tumbling, and aerial tricks. These mats offer more cushioning and shock absorption than floor mats. They are made of thick foam and covered in vinyl.

Spring floors make it safer and easier to perform tumbling skills.

Some gyms have a safety pit to help cheerleaders practice their stunts and landings. A cheer safety pit is a large foam block. It is much thicker than a landing mat but also much more expensive, often costing more than $1,000.

Shaped training mats help cheerleaders practice tumbling skills. These mats roll with a cheerleader across the gym floor. They help cheerleaders learn to position their bodies for tumbling skills. One common type of shaped mat is an octagon tumbling mat. Incline mats are another type of shaped training mat. These mats are triangular. Shaped mats help cheerleaders practice tumbling skills such as walkovers and handsprings.

Many cheer gyms have spring floors. This type of floor has springs underneath the surface. The springs absorb shocks and provide a softer landing surface than a bare floor. A cheerleader who falls during a stunt can be seriously injured. Spring floors used with landing mats can help prevent severe injuries from falls.

!

PROTECTIVE HEADGEAR

Aerial tricks can be dangerous. To reduce the risk of injury, some cheerleaders wear protective headgear at practice. Protective headgear may look like a padded helmet or headband. If a cheerleader falls, this headgear gives protection by absorbing some of the impact.

TRAINING TOOLS

Strength training helps cheerleaders build strong muscles for stunts and tumbling. It also helps them build enough stamina to perform complex routines. Free weights, medicine balls, and strength training machines can help with strength training. Most of these tools can be found in gyms, but cheerleaders can also purchase weights to work out at home.

Other tools help cheerleaders improve their flexibility and balance. Stretching straps help cheerleaders perform flexibility exercises and learn to position their bodies properly during routines. Stunt stands are small raised platforms that let cheerleaders practice balancing in different positions in the air.

Cheerleaders spend hours practicing routines, stunts, and tumbling skills. They have many tools to help them. Using the right gear and tools can help cheerleaders build strength and safely master their routines.

Strength training can help cheerleaders prevent injuries.

CHAPTER 4

PROPS

Props can make a cheerleading routine eye catching and exciting. Cheerleaders use props to show spirit and attract a crowd's attention. There are many different props that cheerleaders can use to make a routine dazzle.

SHOWING SPIRIT

Poms are among the most recognizable cheerleading props. Poms are made of colorful plastic or foil strips. The strips are

Cheerleaders can pair poms with dance moves, stunts, and jumps to make the skills more exciting.

Cheerleaders should stand still while using megaphones so the devices can better project their voices.

attached to a handle. Poms usually match a team's colors. Cheerleaders hold poms in their hands as they dance, using the poms to accentuate their movements. Some cheerleaders may use smaller poms called shakers. Cheerleaders shake poms and shakers to build a crowd's excitement.

Megaphones are cone-shaped props that project a cheerleader's voice. Cheerleaders use megaphones to lead chants and cheers. This helps audiences hear cheerleaders during loud games.

These props are often decorated with a team's colors or a picture of the team's mascot.

Flip signs can be used to lead cheers and chants. The signs are big, with words printed on both sides. Cheerleaders hold up the signs to tell the crowd what to cheer. This helps get the crowd involved and excited.

Cheerleaders may also wave flags and carry banners. These show team and school support and help catch a crowd's attention. They may have inspiring words written on them to help motivate a team.

PROPS AT COMPETITIONS

Cheerleaders performing at competitions should check the event's rules before including props in their routines. Some competitions allow only poms. Others allow props to be used during certain skills but not during others.

THE RIGHT PROPS

Cheer teams should look for props that match their style. Some props can be customized to match a team's colors. If a team can't find the perfect prop, they can try to make their own. Tutorials online teach people to make signs and poms.

Props must also be safe. They should not have sharp edges, as these could cause injuries. Props must also be the correct size. Props that are too big or heavy can be difficult to handle, while props that are too small may be hard to see from the audience. Props should also be durable. They must withstand hours of practice and performances without breaking or looking dull.

Cheerleading is a difficult activity, but having the right tools can make it easier. With the right uniform, training supplies, and props, cheerleaders can learn to perform incredible routines. Seeing these routines come together makes the hard work worth it.

Cheerleading can be a hobby, a career, or both.

GLOSSARY

cohesive
Working or fitting together well.

coordinated
Moving and speaking together, often by using a shout, motion, or device.

customized
Made for a specific person or team.

mascot
A symbol such as an animal, object, or historical figure that represents a team.

prop
An object such as a pom-pom, flag, or megaphone that is used to enhance a cheerleader's routine.

routine
A performance made up of individual stunts, tumbling moves, jumps, and dance moves.

squad
A cheerleading team.

stamina
The ability to perform physical exercise for an extended time.

stunt
A skill in which a cheerleader is supported above the ground by one or more teammates.

tumbling
Gymnastics skills such as cartwheels and flips.

MORE INFORMATION

BOOKS

Mooney, Carla. *Competitive Cheerleading*. Abdo, 2025.

Roggio, Sarah. *Strength Training*. Abdo, 2025.

Troupe, Thomas Kingsley. *Cheerleading*. Crabtree, 2022.

ONLINE RESOURCES

To learn more about cheerleading tools and gear, please visit abdobooklinks.com or scan this QR code. These links are routinely monitored and updated to provide the most current information available.

INDEX

ABOUT THE AUTHOR

Carla Mooney is a graduate of the University of Pennsylvania with a degree in economics. Today, she writes for young people and is the author of many books for young adults and children.